First Violin Concerto
and
Scottish Fantasy
in Full Score

MAX BRUCH

Dover Publications, Inc.
New York

Bibliographical Note

This Dover edition, first published in 1994, is an unabridged republication in one volume of two works originally published separately. C. F. W. Siegel's Musikalienhandlung, Leipzig, originally published Max Bruch's *Concert für die Violine (Vorspiel, Adagio und Finale), Op. 26* (n.d.). N. Simrock, G.m.b.H. in Berlin originally published Bruch's *Fantasie (Einleitung—Adagio—Scherzo—Andante—Finale) für die Violine mit Orchester und Harfe unter freier Benutzung schottischer Volksmelodieen, Op. 46* (1880). The original title page of the Concerto carries the inscription "Joseph Joachim in Freundschaft zugeeignet"; that of the Fantasy, the inscription "Seinem Freunde Pablo de Sarasate zugeeignet."

The Dover edition adds lists of instrumentation and contents (including the complete original subheading of each work), translates three German movement and section headings, and makes minor corrections in the scores.

Library of Congress Cataloging-in-Publication Data

Bruch, Max, 1838–1920.
    [Concerto, violin, orchestra, no. 1, op. 26, G minor]
    First violin concerto, op. 26 ; and, Scottish fantasy, op. 46 / Max Bruch.—In full score.
    1 score.
    Both works for violin and orchestra.
    First work originally published: Leipzig : C.F.W. Siegel's Musikalienhandlung; second work originally published: Berlin : N. Simrock, 1880.
    ISBN 0-486-28295-3 (pbk.)
    1. Concertos (Violin)—Scores. 2. Violin with orchestra—Scores. I. Bruch, Max, 1838–1920. Schottische Fantasie. II. Title: Scottish fantasy.
M1012.B88 op. 26 1994   94-18595
                                                                 CIP
                                                                 M

Manufactured in the United States of America
Dover Publications, Inc., 31 East 2nd Street, Mineola, N.Y. 11501

Contents

Dedicated in Friendship
to Joseph Joachim

First Violin Concerto
in G Minor

(Prelude, Adagio and Finale)

Op. 26 (1868)

Instrumentation

2 Flutes [Flöten]
2 Oboes [Hoboen]
2 Clarinets in B♭ [Clarinetten (B)]
2 Bassoons [Fagotte]

4 Horns in C, D, E♭, B♭ [Hörner (C, D, Es, B)]
2 Trumpets in D, E♭ [Trompeten (D, Es)]

Timpani [Pauken]

Solo Violin [Violine principale]

Violin 1, 2 [Violine]
Violas [Bratsche]
Cellos [Violoncello]
Basses [Contrabass]

I. Prelude

II.

III. Finale

A

f
p
f
p
p
f
p
p
grazioso
cresc.
f
p dolce
p
f
p dolce
pp
f
p
pp
f
p dolce
pizz.
f
p dolce
pizz.

94   First Violin Concerto (III)

122   First Violin Concerto (III)

Presto.

Scottish Fantasy

for Violin with Orchestra and Harp

(Fantasia, Making Free Use of Scottish Folk Melodies)

Op. 46 (1880)

Instrumentation

2 Flutes [Flauti]
2 Oboes [Oboi]
2 Clarinets in B♭ [Clarinetti (B)]
2 Bassoons [Fagotti]

4 Horns in F [Corni (F)]
2 Trumpets in D, E♭ [Trombe (D, Es)]
3 Trombones [Tromboni]
Tuba [Tuba]

Timpani [Timpani]
Bass Drum & Cymbals [Gran Tamburo e Piatti]

Solo Violin [Violino principale]

Violin I, II [Violino]
Violas [Viola]
Cellos [Violoncello]
Basses [Basso]

Harp [Arpa]

Introduction

I.

II. Scherzo

Solo.

Scottish Fantasy (II)   149

III.

IV. Finale

THE END